# At My
# Grandy's Knee

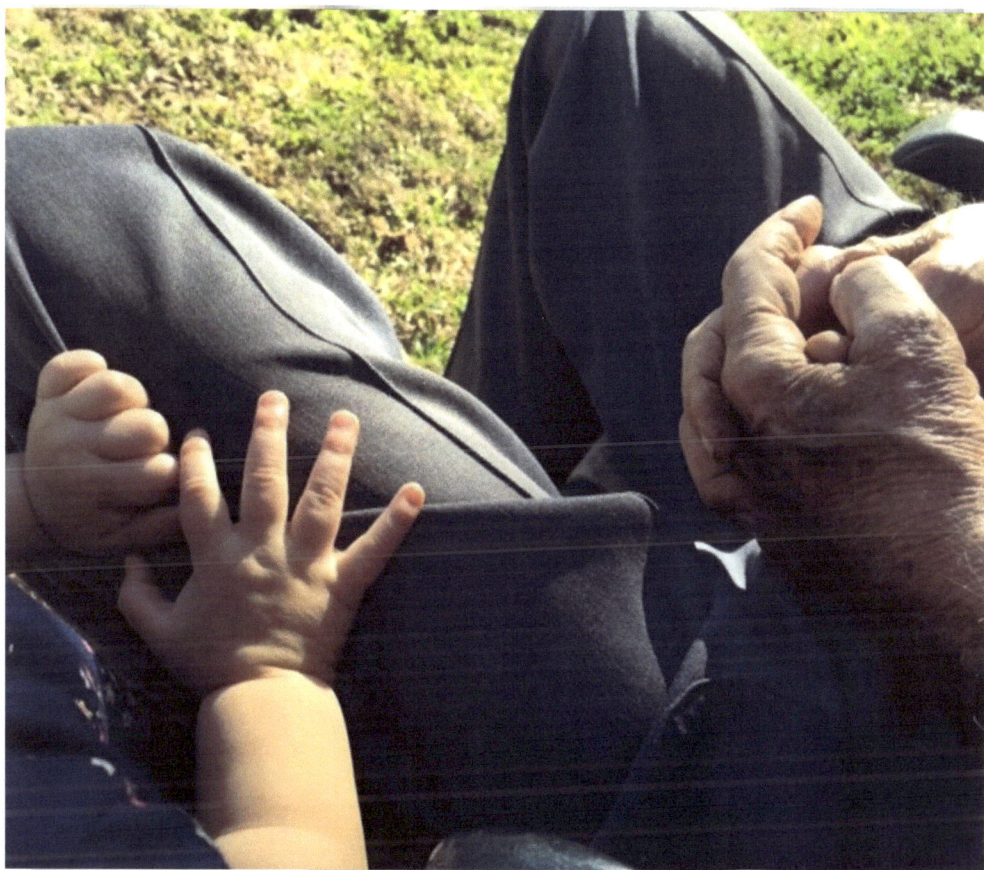

## by Jeryl Christmas

This Book Belongs To

_____

# Flannel Memories

Special thanks to Lindsay Rowe and Sherry Glenn for their
help with the photography and Meredith Lehnen for making
the precious treasures out of Grandy's flannel shirts.

It's a shame I won't remember
all those moments that took place
as I gazed into the eyes
of that 90-year-old face.

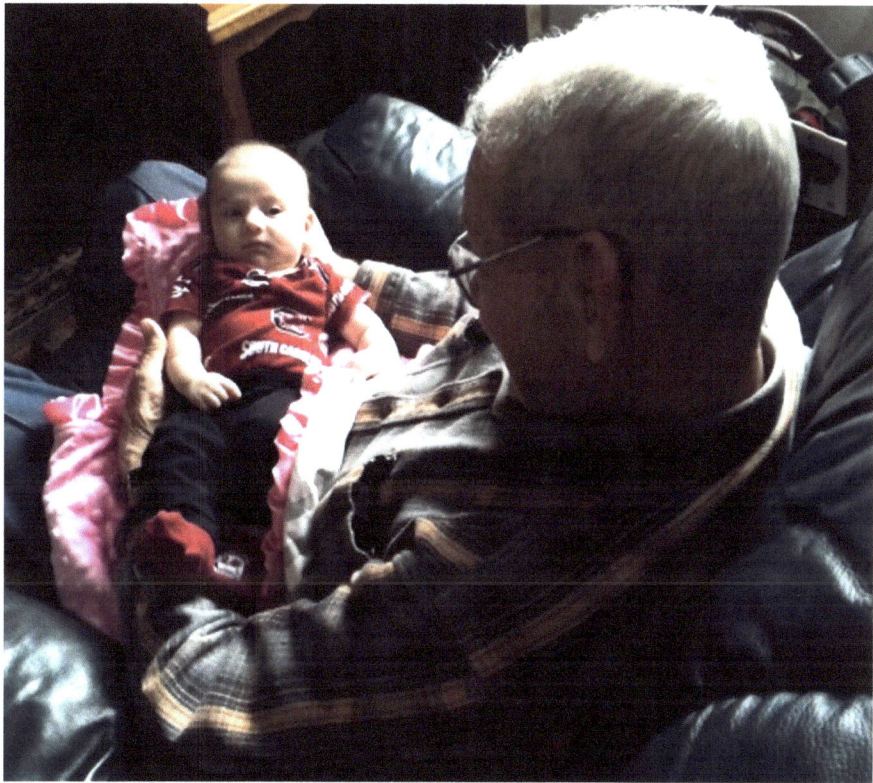

Oh, the things I bet he told me—
the things I'd love to see,
if I could just remember
being at my grandy's knee.

Each story from the past,
like a pretty patchwork quilt,
is interwoven through the ages
on which my life is built.

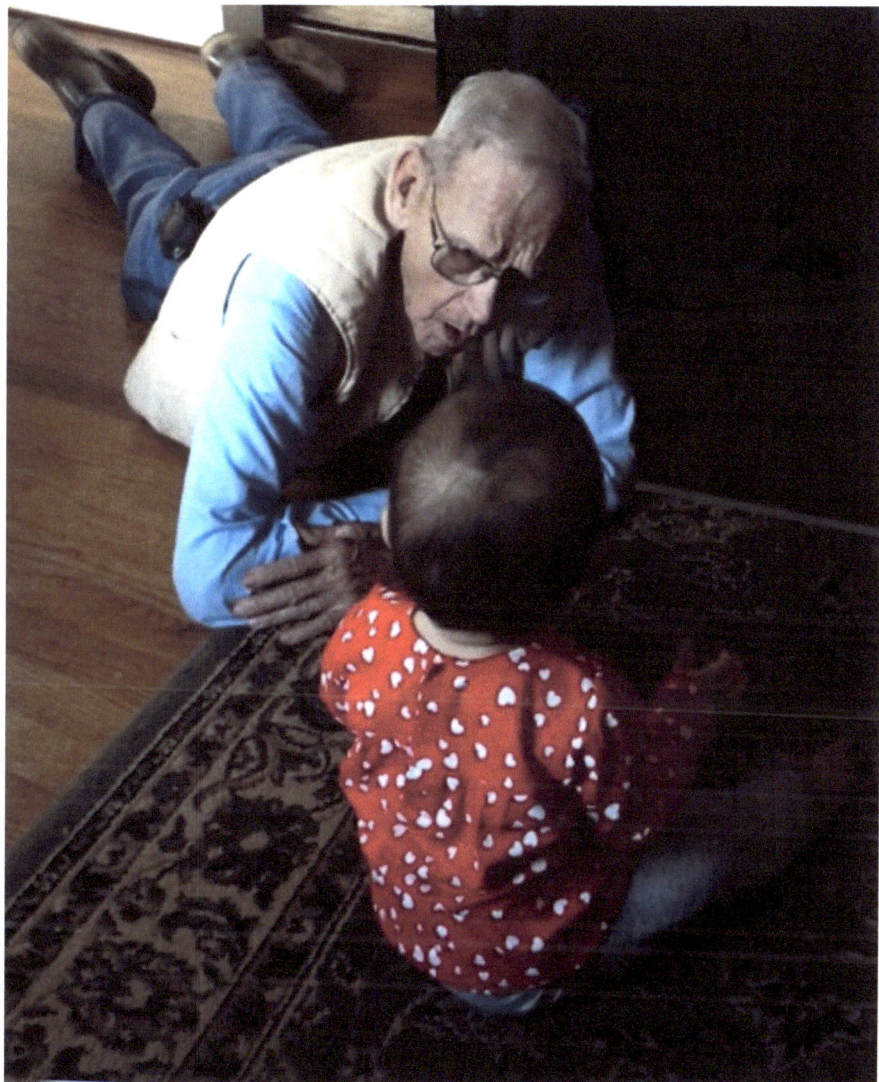

Did I listen so intently?
Did I turn and lend an ear?
I hope I took advantage
of that time that was so dear.

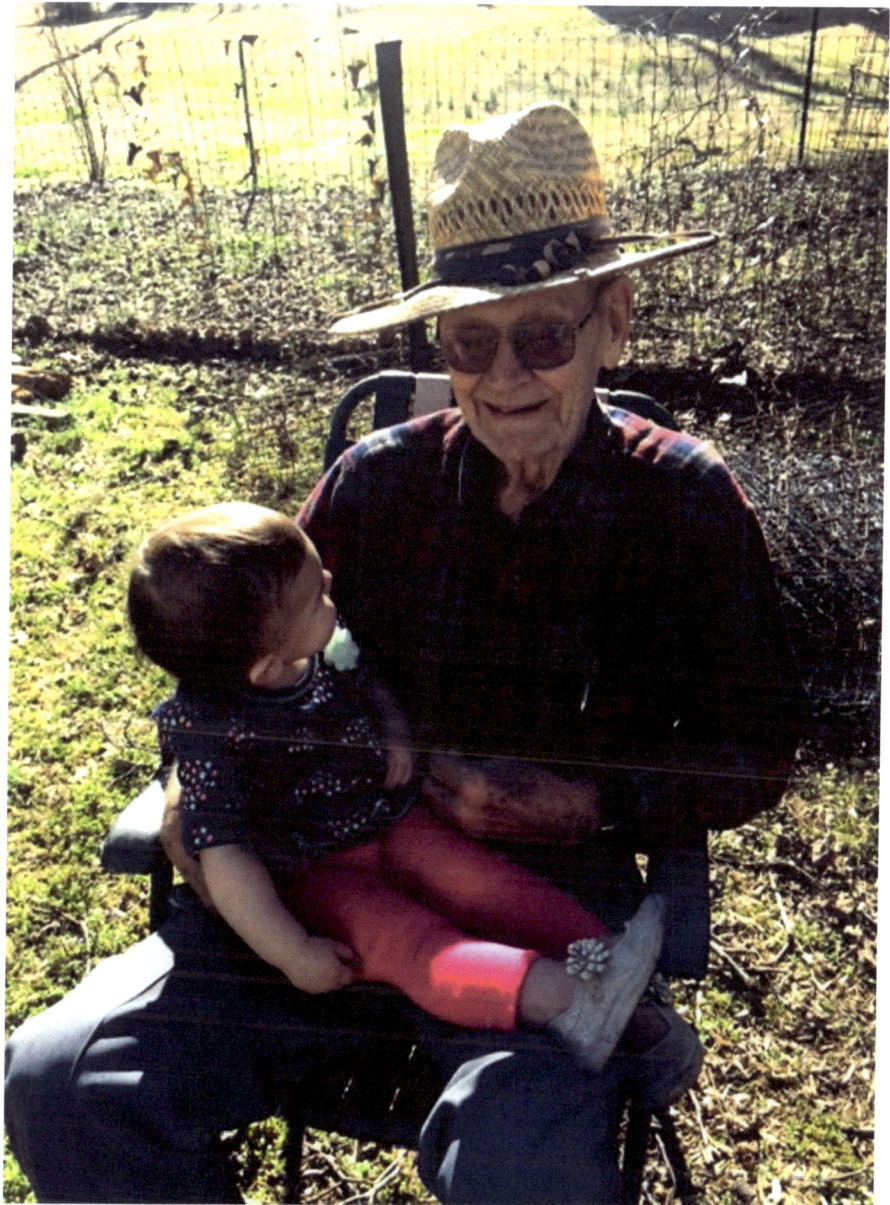

His garden was his haven
grown with patient, loving hands—
hands toughened and so weathered
from working on his land.

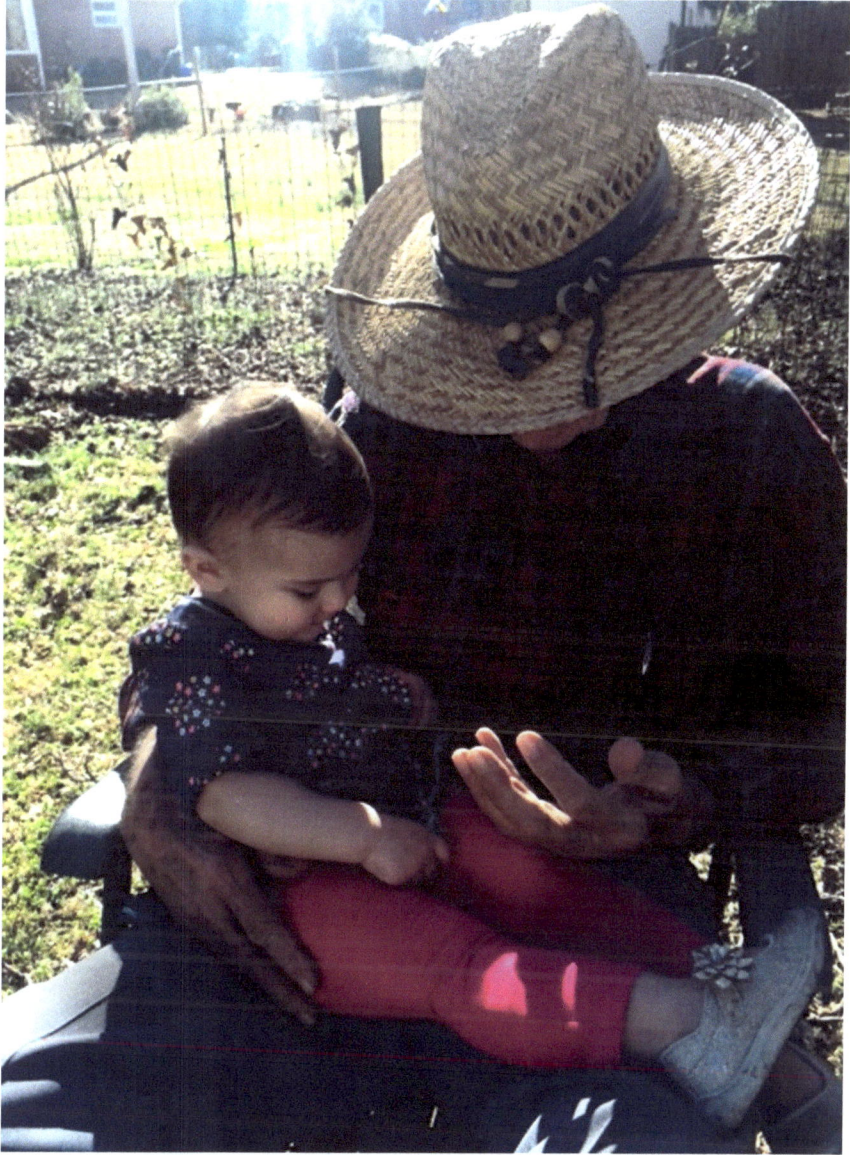

As I think about my future,
I'll keep in mind my past
and the legacy he left me
that no one can surpass.

I heard he never struggled
to attain great wealth or fame,
but with pride he'd introduce himself
with "Jackson is my name."

Now he's gone, but not forgotten,
and often it still hurts,
so Gram had priceless treasures made
from Grandy's well-worn shirts.

It's funny how life's cycle works.

For when my brother came,

I think my grandy wanted him

to carry on his name.

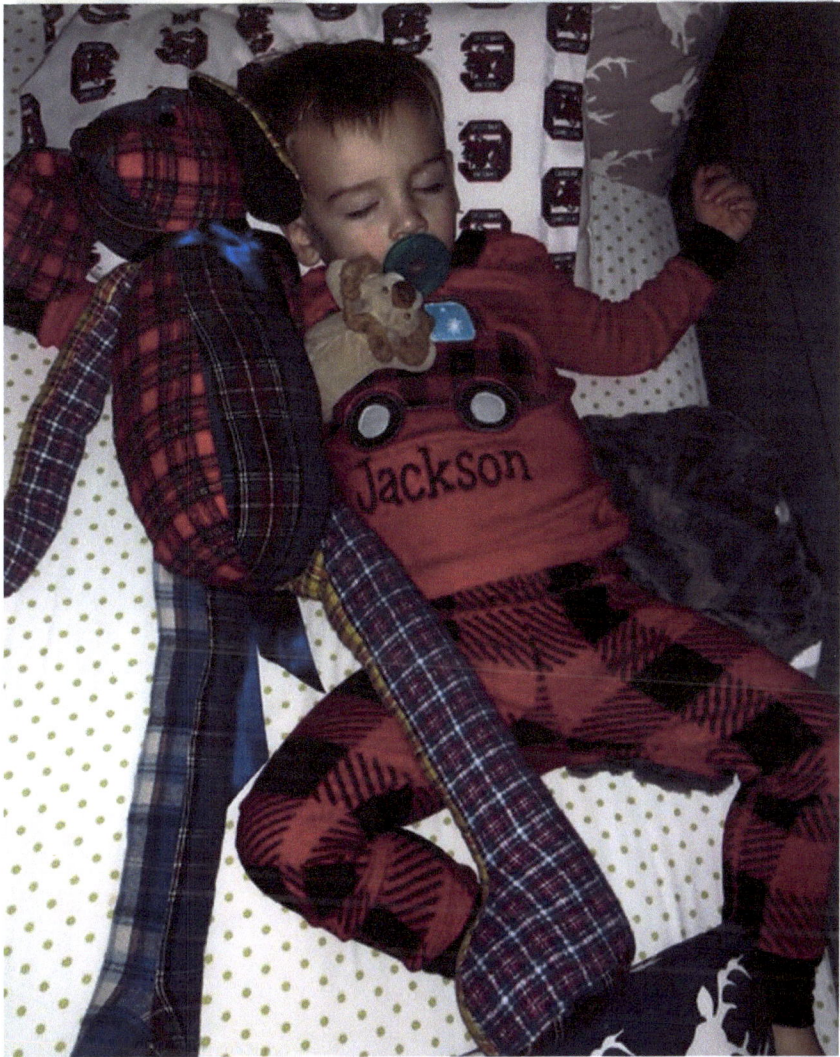

I hope we'll do him justice
and follow in his ways
of honoring God and family
like he did for all his days.

# Thomas Edward Jackson

# Jackson Edward Rowe

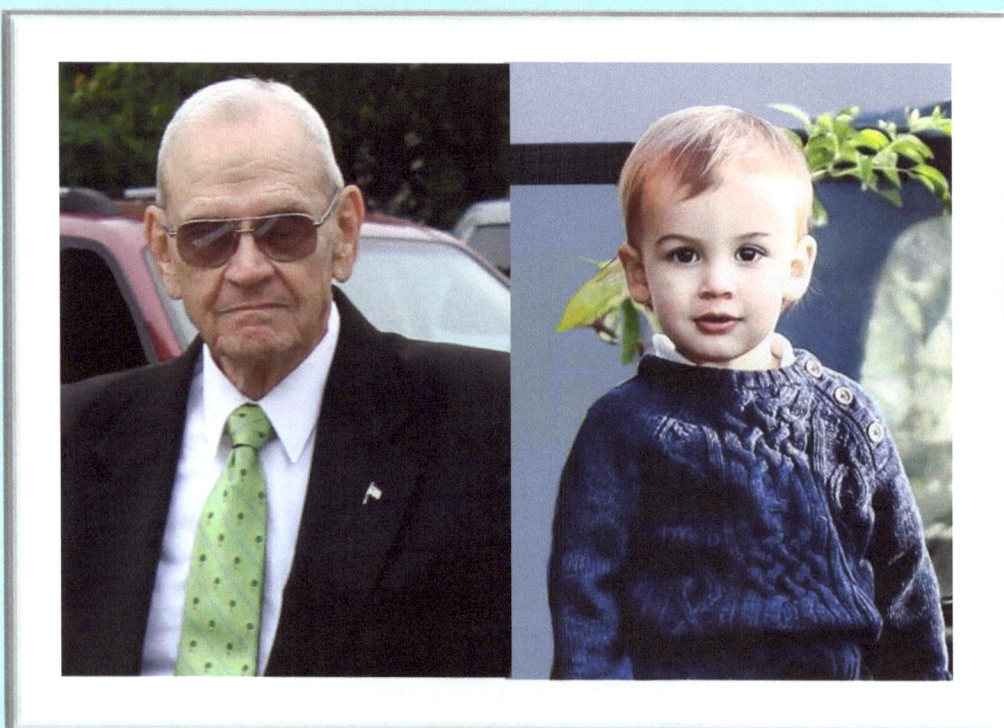

# Life's cycle will continue
## as onward it will go ...

Courtesy of Joe Jackson Photography

www.ingramcontent.com/pod-product-compliance
Lightning Source LLC
Chambersburg PA
CBHW042110040426
42448CB00002B/211